Whiteboard Active

Rites of Passage

Whiteboard Active

Whiteboard Active contains the best of BBC video alongside pictures, text and activities to provide you and your pupils with unforgettable lessons.

Technical support and installation directions, as well as a full introduction to the features, tools and navigation, can be found in the booklet inside the CD-ROM case and via the help button that appears at the top of each screen.

This teacher's book contains support and further information on each unit of the CD-ROM.

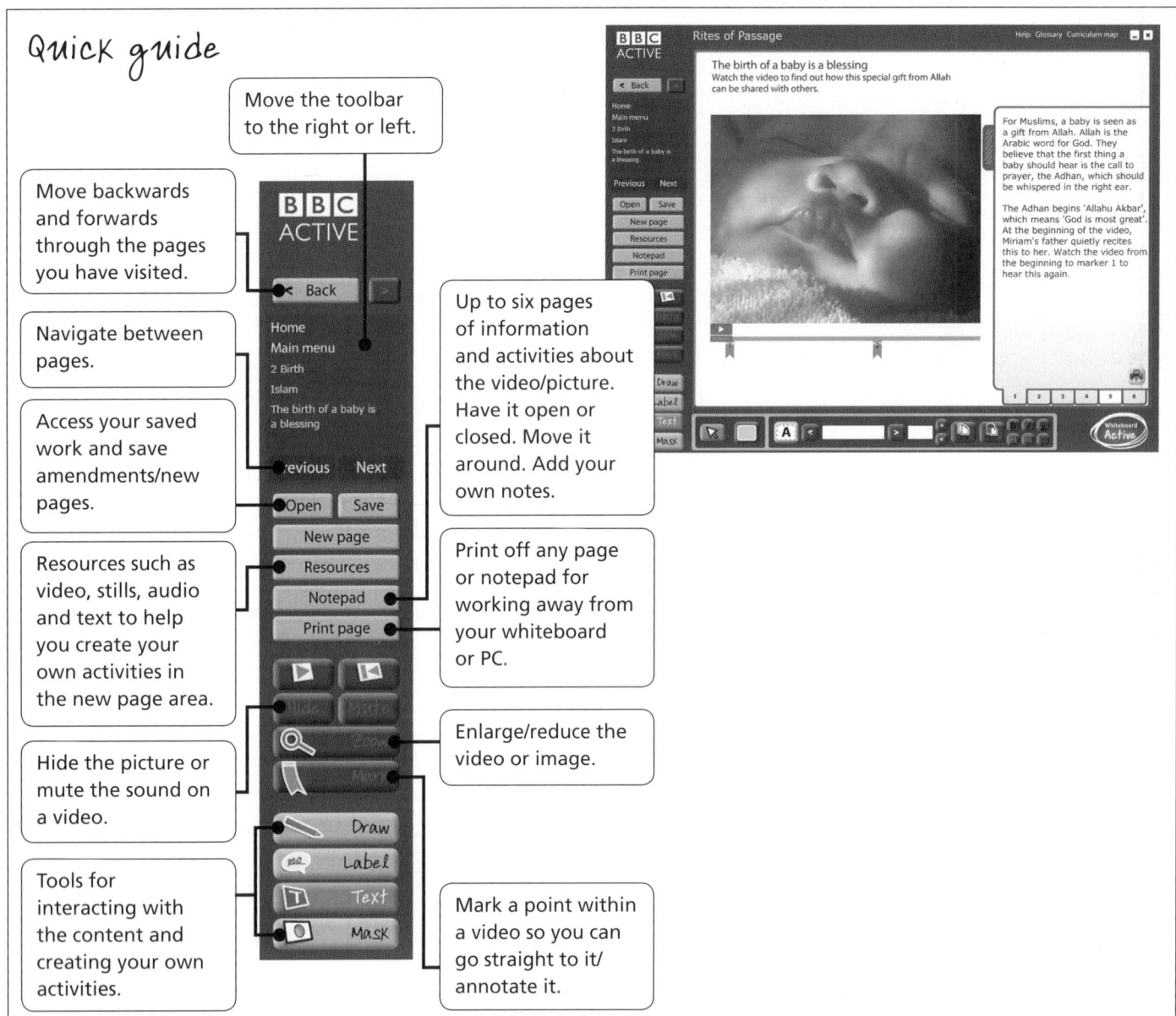

Quick guide

Move the toolbar to the right or left.

Move backwards and forwards through the pages you have visited.

Navigate between pages.

Access your saved work and save amendments/new pages.

Resources such as video, stills, audio and text to help you create your own activities in the new page area.

Hide the picture or mute the sound on a video.

Tools for interacting with the content and creating your own activities.

Up to six pages of information and activities about the video/picture. Have it open or closed. Move it around. Add your own notes.

Print off any page or notepad for working away from your whiteboard or PC.

Enlarge/reduce the video or image.

Mark a point within a video so you can go straight to it/ annotate it.

How to use Whiteboard Active

The notepad: you will find a comprehensive range of activities, questions and information in the notepad – *always open the notepad to see what is inside.*

Some suggestions

• Watch or listen to the video with either the sound or picture off and ask pupils to describe what they think is happening. Then turn the picture or sound back on and ask how it changes their understanding.

• Ask pupils to identify/highlight features on screen using the draw tools.

• Use the mask tools to focus on part of an image or to slowly reveal an image. Can pupils guess what it is?

• Create labels for pupils to move to the correct part of an image. Alternatively, ask pupils to create their own labels.

• Write descriptions, questions and answers on screen using the text tool.

• Open the resource folder and drag images, video clips and audio files onto a new page to create your own activities, or ask pupils to do so.

• Print any screen or notepad.

Writing focus

The 'Writing focus' pages offer cross-curricular writing activities. They can be used when teaching both Religious Education and literacy, as they offer exciting contexts for writing and provide examples of different genres.

The activities include:

- a range of writing tasks that span a variety of genres
- tools to complete the task
- key facts for pupils to remember when writing a report/letter/diary account, etc.
- keywords.

They are designed to support the following strands of the Renewed Literacy Strategy:

Write a wide range of texts on paper and on screen

Strand 9: Creating and shaping texts

- Write independently and creatively for purpose, pleasure and learning
- Use and adapt a range of forms, suited to different purposes and readers
- Make stylistic choices, including vocabulary, literary features and viewpoint or voice
- Use structural and presentational features for meaning and impact

Strand 10: Text structure and organisation

- Organise ideas into coherent structures, including layout, sections and paragraphs
- Write cohesive paragraphs, linking sentences within and between them

Strand 11: Sentence structure and punctuation

- Vary and adapt sentence structure for meaning and effect
- Convey meaning through grammatically accurate and correctly punctuated sentences

Strand 12: Presentation

- Use keyboard skills and ICT tools confidently to compose and present work.

The CD-ROM

The CD-ROM has a simple structure and can be used in many ways. As well as supporting work with the whole class, it can be used in other parts of your lesson. Groups, pairs or individuals can use the CD-ROM itself or work on printed activities that you can create using a new page.

The CD-ROM is divided into five units. These are listed on the main menu and on the contents page of this Teacher's book.

Each unit is divided into pages, each with a specific objective. The content of the pages varies widely and includes the following:

- video clips, which can be viewed at standard size and full-screen, with or without the notepad in view
- photographs and stills from the video clips
- audio files and slideshows
- interactive activities
- 'new page' area, which allows you to create your own new page using any of the video clips, audio files and image resources from *Rites of Passage*.

NB For more information about different ways to interact with the videos (and all the other page types) using the Whiteboard Active tools, please see the booklet inside the CD-ROM case.

Religious Education (RE) is a compulsory subject for schools across the UK. The teaching content varies according to whether or not a school has a religious character and where the school is located within the UK – schools are required to teach according to local and national guidelines.

In Scotland, RE is called Religious and Moral Education from 5 to 14 and Religious, Moral and Philosophical Studies from 14 to 18. National guidelines state expectations of student learning and inform the local authority when it draws up a curriculum for each school.

Religious Education in England and Wales follows statute laid down by the 1944 Education Act and more recently amended by the Education Reform Act 1988 and the Education Act 2000. It is the only subject in England mentioned in statute. Parents have the right to withdraw their children from RE. Each local authority has a Local Agreed Syllabus that sets out the statutory curriculum for its schools at each key stage.

Religious Education taught in faith schools may be set out by the local diocese or by the school in partnership with its faith community and governing body. This may be influenced by a trust deed.

In Northern Ireland, schools have to provide RE in accordance with the core syllabus drawn up by the four main churches and specified by the Department of Education.

In England, local syllabuses for RE may be based on the Qualifications and Curriculum Authority (QCA) Non-statutory National Framework for Religious Education (2004), which provides guidelines for the provision of RE at all key stages and models the eight levels as applied in National Curriculum subjects. This document does not influence RE syllabuses in Wales, Scotland or Northern Ireland.

Religious Education in the curriculum

'Religious Education provokes challenging questions about the ultimate meaning and purpose of life, beliefs about God, the self and the nature of reality, issues of right and wrong and what it means to be human.

'It develops pupils' knowledge and understanding of Christianity, other principal religions, other religious traditions and other world views that offer answers to questions such as these.

'It offers opportunities for personal reflection and spiritual development.

'It enhances pupils' awareness and understanding of religions and beliefs, teachings, practices and forms of expression, as well as of the influence of religion on individuals, families, communities and cultures.

'Religious Education encourages pupils to learn from different religions, beliefs, values and traditions while exploring their own beliefs and questions of meaning. It challenges pupils to reflect on, consider, analyse, interpret and evaluate issues of truth, belief, faith and ethics and to communicate their responses.

'Religious Education encourages pupils to develop their sense of identity and belonging. It enables them to flourish individually within their communities and as citizens in a pluralistic society and global community.

'Religious Education has an important role in preparing pupils for adult life, employment and lifelong learning. It enables pupils to develop respect for and sensitivity to others, in particular those whose faiths and beliefs are different from their own. It promotes discernment and enables pupils to combat prejudice.'

QCA Non-Statutory National Framework for RE

At Key Stage 2 (age 7-11), across the UK, pupils usually learn about Christianity and one or more other major religions, recognising the impact of religion and belief on the lives of individuals locally, nationally and internationally.

At this key stage, pupils learn about sacred texts and other sources of authority and consider their impact on and meaning for believers. They also begin to recognise diversity in religion, learning about similarities and differences both within and between religions and beliefs and the importance of dialogue between them.

As pupils extend their use of RE specialist vocabulary, they develop greater ability to communicate their knowledge and ideas.

Pupils should learn to recognise the challenges involved in distinguishing between ideas of 'right' and 'wrong', valuing what is good and true and recognising other people's viewpoints. Knowledge of the religions they study and recognition of the importance that religion plays in people's lives will help pupils to develop respect and foster responsible attitudes in the community. Through active involvement, pupils will explore the spiritual and moral dimensions of RE in order to consider their own beliefs and values and inform their own search for meaning and purpose.

Two aspects of RE

There are two commonly recognised aspects of RE. These are:

- **Learning about religion**/Exploring religious beliefs, teachings and practice(s)
- **Learning from religion**/Expressing personal responses.

Most syllabuses recognise that RE is not merely about acquiring knowledge and understanding about religions; it also incorporates an opportunity for pupils to reflect and respond to what they have learnt. In Wales, this is described as 'exploring religious beliefs, teachings and practices' and 'expressing personal responses'. The two attainment targets for RE in England are described by the Qualifications and Curriculum Authority (QCA):

AT1: *'Learning about religion includes enquiry into, and investigation of, the nature of religion. It focuses on beliefs, teachings and sources, practices and ways of life and forms of expression. It includes the skills of interpretation, analysis and explanation. Pupils learn to communicate their knowledge and understanding using specialist vocabulary. It includes identifying and developing an understanding of ultimate questions and ethical issues.'*

AT2: *'Learning from religion is concerned with developing pupils' reflection on, and response to, their own experiences and learning about religion. It develops pupils' skills of application, interpretation and evaluation of what they learn about religion, particularly questions of identity and belonging, meaning, purpose, truth, values and commitments, and communicating their responses.'*

Throughout this CD-ROM, activities to support both the knowledge base for the subject and the affective, reflective aspect of RE have been included.

Every Child Matters

Every Child Matters: Change for Children is a new approach to the well-being of children and young people from birth to age 19. The challenge is for each school to identify how it can contribute to this. The Government's aim is for all children, whatever their background or circumstances, to have the support they need to:

- be healthy
- stay safe
- enjoy and achieve
- make a positive contribution
- achieve economic well-being.

Religious Education can make a particular contribution to all of these aims.

Key principles

For RE to be meaningful, pupils need to feel free and comfortable when talking about the place of religious experience in their own lives. To support this, it is necessary to foster an environment where pupils can appreciate that everyone is of equal importance, where diversity is celebrated and where pupils can develop an understanding that the needs of everyone should be treated fairly and equally. Within such an environment, cultural and religious diversity is regarded as positive, and pupils can feel that they are able to express their viewpoints and beliefs in safety.

It is not the purpose of RE to convert pupils to any particular belief system or faith. Religious Education supports pupils in reflecting on the place of religious belief and experience in humanity as a whole and in their own lives and communities. This CD-ROM does not assume that pupils will approach the subject from a position of committed faith or that teachers or pupils have background knowledge of the religions covered.

Rites of Passage CD-ROM

'Rites of passage' is an important topic in Religious Education. The phrase refers to rituals, ceremonies or celebrations that occur at key moments in people's lives. They tend to mark transitional moments; the 'passage' from one stage of life to another. Generally, the occasion has significance not only for the individual but also for the family and community (e.g. baptism). Not all key moments are marked in a religious way, as in the case of eighteenth and twenty-first birthday parties. However, for birth, marriage and death, religious rites are common throughout the world.

The material on this CD-ROM will enable schools to explore what happens at many rites of passage in the UK and to discover and respond to the thoughts and feelings of the people involved. The video clips offer a privileged opportunity to see at close quarters rites of passage that are often deeply moving or joyfully celebratory.

Some syllabuses may not include the phrase 'Rites of passage'. The topic chart on pages 7 to 8 indicates the content of the CD-ROM, so you can make up your own syllabus links with the material.

Teaching about life's end and afterwards

Although loss, death and bereavement affect everyone, this area of human experience remains one that many people find most difficult to discuss. It is therefore very important that teachers plan for the introduction of this topic carefully, developing sensitive foundations and support networks in school so that pupils can experience a secure environment where they can articulate their views and feelings, developing a vocabulary and feeling able to consider and accommodate views that differ from their own without finding this too challenging or disturbing. This will best be provided in a school where the ethos supports pupils' personal development and where teachers, parents and the wider community are united in their concern for every child.

Religious Education subject leaders should be aware that adults in school may also be experiencing personal loss or find it difficult to address these topics without support. Parents should be informed in advance that this topic is going to be introduced and teachers should ensure they are aware of possible personal experiences that may make the topic difficult for anyone in the class. It may be that special consideration needs to be given to making links between the pastoral support available for staff and pupils and the teaching of this topic in order that it can be delivered effectively.

Dealing with the topic of death and how people make sense of the experience can help to create a caring and supportive community that will help members to deal with personal loss long after this unit of work is over. An example of this occurred with the class of children seen sharing experiences of special things that remind them of people they have lost (*Helping us to remember*). After filming, one of the children in the class sadly died. The class found that the work they had been doing gave them a vocabulary to share and discuss the loss of their classmate and made the situation easier for the school and their families to support. The family of the child who died wanted the video to be used to reinforce their own view that the topic had been more than just RE – it had helped the children to develop skills for their whole lives.

Handling questions

Many teachers are concerned about responding to unexpected questions or comments in a whole-class situation, usually because they lack confidence in their own knowledge of world faiths. If a teacher does not know the answer to a question, there is nothing wrong in saying so. The teacher and pupil can research the question together or the teacher can promise to pass the question on to someone else who can help them to find the answer.

Handling issues of religious diversity

Different religions and cultures have their own truth claims. However, it is a mistake to assume that all members of a particular religious group will have the same beliefs or practice their beliefs in the same way. The best advice is not to make any assumptions. Talk to pupils and find out where they stand, what their needs are, what constraints they are under and how best to work with them. Effective communication with parents, carers and the wider community is crucial in developing a shared awareness and understanding of cultural and religious sensitivities.

Teachers will need to guard against:

- Attributing particular behaviours or attitudes to faiths or cultures
- Stereotyping members of faiths by equating culture or nationality with faith and/or expecting believers to behave in particular ways
- Inter-cultural and interfaith attitudes coming from the children's homes
- Using language that implies that everyone believes the same thing or celebrates a rite of passage in the same way.

Vocabulary

Lists of useful vocabulary can be found in the glossary on the CD-ROM. The acquisition of correct terminology is part of good RE. Please note that, as many of the words used in religions originate in languages other than English, there may be variations in their spelling, as many are transliterations. Spellings used on this CD-ROM are those recommended in the Religious Education Glossary published by the Quality and Curriculum Authority. This is available from the QCA website.

The significance of this CD-ROM for RE

Many CDs are available that provide the basic facts about topics such as welcoming someone into a community, becoming a full member of a faith or weddings. The richness of this CD-ROM lies in that it goes far beyond facts and information, although these are included. The video clips, drawn from BBC programmes, enable the user to observe individuals and communities engaged in personal and family celebrations and, in interviews or commentaries, to see them share their thoughts and feelings about faith and the meaning of the experience to them.

Many teachers find it difficult to resource and explore the more affective, non-factual aspects of RE. These are expressed in Attainment Target 2 and are in the areas of personal response, reflection, interpretation and evaluation.

This CD-ROM offers extensive opportunities for such classroom activity, stimulated chiefly by the believers from the faiths represented who have generously allowed filming in their places of worship and homes, and who have spoken about their personal responses in both film and audio recordings.

In addition to the input from religious communities, activities have been devised to encourage pupils' engagement with and responses to the subject matter.

Topic chart

Units	Religious Education topics	Content
Unit 1: Introduction	Occasions for family gatherings and celebrations	Images of some important times in life: birth, birthdays, marriage, death
	Growing old	Perspectives on different ages in life
	Searching for happiness	What gives purpose and fulfilment?
Unit 2: Birth	Celebrating a new life	Ways of welcoming a new baby
	Islam – welcoming a baby	Head-shaving, prayer and charitable giving
	The significance of names	Names and identity
	Sikhism – choosing a name	Gurdwara worship The Guru Granth Sahib
	Christianity – Baptism	Church worship
	Symbolism – water, light	Anglican infant baptism
	Promises	Family celebrations The Church family
	Jesus' dedication at the Temple Jesus as a special baby	The story of Jesus being acknowledged by Anna and Simeon as God's promised 'light for the world'
Unit 3: Growing up	Change and impermanence	Moving to a new school
	Bar mitzvah and bat mitzvah	Taking responsibility in the community
	Coming of age	Synagogue Rabbi Torah
	Roman Catholic First Communion	Becoming full members of the Church Priest
	Mass, Holy Communion, Eucharist	Bread and wine
	Confirmation in the Church of England	Confirming baptismal vows Bishop
	Christianity – adult baptism	Jesus' baptism in the river Jordan Baptism by total immersion
	Adult baptism in a Baptist church	The symbol of water as spiritual cleansing or new life and of death and resurrection
	Sikhism – the story of the Khalsa	Guru Gobind Singh and the founding of the Khalsa
	Taking amrit	The ceremony when people commit themselves to living as true Sikhs
	The Five Ks	The symbolism of the five Ks and their meaning in daily life: Kara, Kaccha, Kesh, Kirpan and Kangha

Units	Religious Education topics	Content
Unit 4: Marriage	Marriage – a rite of passage around the world	Different weddings customs Family and community celebrations
	Christianity – marriage ceremonies	Vows
	Christianity – the story of Jesus at a wedding Miracles The Bible	Jesus turns water into wine The Bible
	Judaism – a wedding	A synagogue ceremony
	Judaism – the story of Ruth and Boaz Models to follow in sacred texts Love and commitment	The Hebrew Bible
	Hinduism – a wedding	An 'arranged' marriage
	Hinduism – the story of Rama and Sita Ancient myths and stories	Rama and Sita as role models of faithfulness and love
Unit 5: The end of the journey	Death – the end of the journey of life	
	Hinduism – beliefs about death	Hindu cremation
	Hinduism – cremation practices	Rajiv Gandhi's state funeral
	Buddhism – beliefs about life and death	The story of the Buddha and the 'four sights' The story of the Buddha and Kisa and the mustard seeds
	Christianity – Christian beliefs about death and life after death	Easter and the belief that Jesus conquered death What Christians believe happens when someone dies The story of the 'Water bugs and dragonflies' Graveyards as places of rest and memory A Christian funeral
	Marking and celebrating the end of a life	The Queen Mother's state funeral
	Memories and memorials	How people are helped to remember

The journey of life

The purpose of this sequence of four video clips is to stimulate thought and responses about ways in which some key moments of life are celebrated or marked. They are: birth, birthdays, marriage and death.

There is no commentary, providing scope to explore the likely feelings and moods in each case. With the exception of the graveyard, the images are not religious. This is to make the responses as inclusive as possible, so that all the class, whether from religious backgrounds or not, will have the opportunity to contribute and share their own thoughts and experiences.

Pupils will no doubt be able to add other celebratory moments that are marked in life. These may include wedding anniversaries and key birthdays, such as the eighteenth, twenty-first and hundredth.

Page 6 of the notepad suggests asking pupils to each draw a timeline representing their own life. They mark on it key birthdays and special moments that they hope will happen, such as special achievements (e.g. passing a driving test) or occasions (e.g. getting engaged or moving to a new house).

Growing old

A series of images, representing different stages in life, is accompanied by children's comments. It is recommended that you first show the slideshow without listening to the commentary. This can be done by clicking the mute button.

Invite the class to look at each image and think, write down or say what was/is/will be best or worst about each age. Which is the best age of all? Why?

Talk about growing old. When do we get old? How old is 'old'? What are pupils looking forward to about getting older? Are there any things they are worried about or afraid of in the future?

You may wish to ask everyone to bring into school pictures of older members of their families and to talk or write about 'being old'.

One likely outcome is to broaden understanding of and empathy towards elderly people.

What makes people happy?

This drag-and-drop activity will encourage thought and response on the theme of happiness. Six thumbnail images are provided, representing answers that children have given in a survey about what makes people happy. They are: money, health, being loved, fame, pets and friends.

In addition, the image of a question mark has been provided in case anyone suggests something else.

Before using the whiteboard for the activity, it is suggested that pupils make their choices either on their own or in pairs/groups. This page could be printed off for everyone to have a copy. Vote on each image to establish where in a hierarchy the class would put it. Then drag and drop the words on the whiteboard for all to see.

Talk about happiness. Can we tell if someone is happy?

You may wish to introduce the place of religious belief in the happiness or contentment felt by many people. All religions place great importance in the search for lasting, inner peace, rather than on material prosperity.

The start of life

This slideshow, with images of how the birth of a baby is greeted by family and friends, introduces the topic of welcoming a baby into the world. The audio explains that planning a family is a common expectation of many couples and then encourages pupils to think about the preparations that take place in the family when a baby is expected.

Teachers will appreciate the need to handle this topic very carefully. Clearly not all babies are planned for and welcomed and this may include members of the class or their siblings. Some babies that are wanted and waited for with great love may arrive very ill, be stillborn or have a life-limiting illness. Therefore, teachers may find using the slideshow without the sound and notepads gives an opportunity to look at this issue in a broader way and perhaps consider the extended family that supports the baby and helps to bring it up. The suggestions for introducing the idea of foster care or adoption (notepad page 5) in relation to Hinduism may help to provide an opportunity to consider the wider 'family' that may share the care of a new baby. You could also invite into the class an adult who is a foster carer or an adoptive parent to talk about the special joy they have experienced helping to care for a baby that is not biologically their own.

It is important to ensure that pupils appreciate that while religious families may consider a baby a gift from God, non-religious families also celebrate the birth of their baby with as much pleasure and gratitude.

A class collection of baby photographs and personal memorabilia will help pupils to engage on a personal level with this topic, and the inclusion of the teacher's own baby photographs will help pupils to appreciate that life's journey goes on into adulthood.

Islam

The birth of a baby is a blessing

Muslims believe a baby is a gift from Allah. Muslims see life as a journey in the sight of and in worship of Allah. They believe that the first thing a baby should hear is the call to prayer, the Adhan, which should be whispered in his or her right ear; no prayers are said to follow this. At the end of a Muslim's life, when a person is taken to a mosque before his or her burial, prayers are said with no call to prayer – the two are linked, showing life's journey as one. You can find out more about the Adhan and prayer in Islam from *Whiteboard Active: Worship and Sacred Places* (BBC Active, 2007).

The ceremony shown takes place seven days after the baby is born. The baby's head is shaved very carefully to show that the child is the servant of Allah. Muslims weigh the hair and give the value of the equivalent weight in gold to charity.

Pupils might like to consider what words they would like to use to welcome a baby into the world.

What's in a name?

The names on this page and their meanings come from a range of cultures. You could use this as an opportunity to explore the naming patterns of different faiths and cultures within the class or school. Our first name is usually chosen for us by our parents or families. Christians call this a Christian name; because not everyone is Christian, a more common way to describe this is as our forename or first name. Our last name is usually a family name or 'surname'. This identifies the family to which we belong.

Pupils might consider how it may be offensive to call the first name of non-Christians a 'Christian' name. They could also investigate how their own names or those of their friends or members of their families were chosen. How difficult might it be to have names that originated with someone very famous or important?

Sikhism

Choosing a name

The video shows happy young Sikh parents who have brought their new baby to their gurdwara, the Sikh place of worship, to thank God for the baby and its health and to get guidance on how to choose the baby's name. It is customary for this to happen within forty days of the baby's birth.

In the video, you see the Guru Granth Sahib being opened and the custom is that the first sound of the reading on the opened page will be the first sound of the new baby's name. Pupils might like to consider how different this naming is from that of many other faiths – the parents have not spent months deliberating over baby names, and at the end of the video they set off to make their minds up at home. Sometimes at this stage, the honour of choosing the baby's name rests with grandparents on one side or the other, so the parents may still have to wait until the older generation have made up their minds.

Most Sikh names are gender-neutral. What defines the name as male or female is the use of 'Singh' for boys or 'Kaur' for girls as a second name. Equality is a cornerstone of Sikhism and so all boys are given the name Singh, which means 'lion', and all girls the name Kaur, which means 'princess'. This shows they are all as important as each other and demonstrates the teaching of the Gurus that caste and religious differences are irrelevant – everyone is equal before God.

Pupils could use the images available in the resource palette to reflect on the feelings of the parents bringing their baby to the gurdwara or to write a card or invitation to the gurdwara to share this experience.

Christianity

A Christian baptism

In this Church of England baptism, you see baby Jamie being brought by his family to be baptised in the family's local church. Baptism is a 'sacrament', a visible sign of God's love. Water is a sign of washing and cleansing. In baptism, it is a sign of being washed free from sin and beginning a new life with God.

Light is an important symbol in the service. A large candle is often lit with the words 'God calls us out of darkness into his marvellous light'. Also, a small presentation candle is given to the person being baptised, or their parents if it is a baby or child. These words are said: 'Shine as a light in the world to the glory of God the Father.'

The promises during baptism are made on behalf of the baby by parents and godparents. However, at confirmation the child takes on these responsibilities. You can see more about this in the **Unit 3: Growing up**. Godparents make the same promises on behalf of the child being baptised as parents do. They promise to pray and support the child and to help the parents bring up the child as a Christian. It is an important and responsible thing to do.

The following words from the service (Common Worship), led by the minister and responded to by the parents and godparents, will be useful if you are introducing this topic with older or more-able pupils; they will also help to engage in a discussion about what parents should be looking for in a godparent – this will act as an introduction for the writing task on the next page, *Writing focus: A big responsibility*.

Minister:

Parents and godparents, the church receives this child/these children with joy.

Today we are trusting God for *their* growth in faith.

Will you pray for *them*,

draw *them* by your example into the community of faith

and walk with *them* in the way of Christ?

Parents and godparents:

With the help of God, we will.

Minister:

In baptism *these children* begin their journey in faith.

You speak for *them* today.

Will you care for *them*?

And help *them* to take *their* place within the life and worship of Christ's Church?

Parents and godparents:

With the help of God, we will.

Often, a baptism service is followed by a family celebration and gifts are given to the baby. Members of the class who have any such gifts might like to describe them and talk about what meaning they have to themselves or their families.

Writing focus: A big responsibility

This writing task is aimed at helping pupils to consider the importance of choosing the right people for the role of being a godparent.

It will help pupils if you begin by making a class list of what the parents might be looking for – perhaps beginning with asking is it important if the godparent is a practising Christian? Do godparents need to belong to the same Christian denomination as the family? What are the responsibilities that fall on godparents? The Church of England recommends that a child should have at least three godparents; they can be family members or friends. However, it is important that the parents choose people who will take an interest in how the child grows up as a Christian and they should be baptised themselves.

You may be able to invite a local Church of England minister in to school to help with this discussion and to give pupils an idea of the way they lead parents in this tricky choice.

Welcome to the Christian family

This page shows Christians from a different part of the Christian family welcoming babies into their community during a dedication service. The service is very busy, with many members of the congregation actively involved.

Pupils will appreciate that the families have made a real effort in their own dress and that of the children being dedicated. In the past, wearing your 'Sunday best' was a common feature of church observance for all denominations – today, this now varies, but on this occasion everyone looks very smart. When pupils consider how the families feel on this occasion, you might like to freeze the video with your own markers so that pupils can consider the expressions of different members of the congregation and families.

The video leads on to the next page, *A welcome for Jesus*, which focuses on Jesus' dedication and makes a strong link between Christian practice and Jesus' life.

A dedication service like this is usually followed by adult baptism at an older age. That is because some Christians believe that baptism should take place when people are old enough to make their own decisions. You will find examples of adult baptism in **Unit 3: Growing up**.

A welcome for Jesus

About 33 days after Jesus' circumcision, or 40 days after his birth, his parents took him to Jerusalem to be dedicated to God. According to Leviticus 12:4-5, every male child was to be brought to the Temple in Jerusalem for dedication to God at the time of his mother's purification. Ritual purification stems back to a Jewish tradition of women being considered unclean after the birth of a child. For forty days for a boy, and sixty days for a girl, women were not allowed to worship in the Temple. At the end of this period, women were brought to the Temple or synagogue to be purified. After the ceremony, they were allowed to take part in religious services again.

The Gospel of Luke (Chapter 2, verses 21 to 38) says that Jesus was met by Anna and Simeon. Simeon was a very religious man and believed he had been told he would see the Messiah before he died. When he saw Jesus, he exclaimed his joy and expectation that Jesus would be a light to the world – Jews and Gentiles alike. His words are called the *Nunc dimittis* in Latin and in the Church of England service (Common Worship) they are expressed as shown opposite.

Now, Lord, you let your servant go in peace: your word has been fulfilled.

My own eyes have seen the salvation which you have prepared in the sight of every people;

A light to reveal you to the nations and the glory of your people Israel.

Some Christians recall this event at a time called Candlemas. This is because at this time, mainly in the Roman Catholic Church, all the candles for the year are blessed. On Candlemas night, many people place lighted candles in their windows at home.

Unit 3: Growing up

Changes and new beginnings

As a springboard for thinking about and responding to change, the focus of this activity is the experience of changing from a primary to a secondary school. In the audio commentary, children, who are soon to leave primary school, look back on earlier years and look ahead to leaving and their new life. They express a mixture of excitement and apprehension as they think of the changes awaiting them.

Before watching the slideshow, click on each image. What do pupils think the slideshow is going to be about? Ask for their thoughts and feelings as they look back and look ahead. You may wish them to list the eight images and then write their ideas down alongside each one. To discuss individual photographs, you can freeze the slideshow and enlarge the image.

You could choose one or more children to read their own thoughts as commentaries to the mute slideshow. Later, after the class have explored their own responses, play the slideshow with the audio track provided. It will be interesting to compare the different views expressed.

Change can be exciting, but also unsettling. Why do people often find change difficult? What changes in life are the most difficult to deal with? What things can help us to feel safe or secure when changes are happening to us? For many people, their religious faith gives them a feeling of security in the midst of change. Some find the Buddhist idea of 'impermanence' helpful – that change is a part of everyone's life: if we expect it, we can accept it more easily.

Judaism

Bar mitzvah: a sign of growing up

Bar mitzvah, which means 'son of the commandment', takes place when Jewish boys are 13 years old. It marks the time when they become adult, responsible members of the Jewish community. During the ceremony, which often takes place in a synagogue, the 'bar mitzvah boy' reads a portion from the Torah scroll in Hebrew. There is usually a family party and gifts given to the new full member of the community.

The video provides opportunities for pointing out features of the synagogue in which this bar mitzvah takes place: the ark and Torah scrolls, the Hebrew text, the rabbi who is teaching Jonathan to read his portion, the yad, or pointer, with which he reads it, the prayer shawl and kippah on people's heads.

Talk about the importance of this occasion to Jonathan. What does it mean to him? Why does he want to have a bar mitzvah?

Bar mitzvah and bat mitzvah ceremonies

A Jewish girl is said to be 'bat mitzvah' or a 'daughter of the commandment' at the age of 12. Liberal or Reformed synagogues honour girls publicly in a similar way to the way they celebrate a boy's bar mitzvah. As the synagogue and family shown in the video are from the Liberal Jewish tradition, Jonathan's older sister, Tanya, had a very similar ceremony to her brother and also read a Torah portion in Hebrew in the synagogue.

Tanya says that she felt proud to read the Torah and that the whole occasion made her feel that she belonged to the Jewish community. What does she mean? Why did she say this?

To become bar or bat mitzvah also means taking responsibility to lead lives in accordance with the principles of the Jewish faith and to be proud to be Jewish. What might this mean? Is it likely to be difficult?

If there are Jewish families in your school or area, would anyone who has had either a bar or bat mitzvah be willing to talk to your class about the occasion and to show any relevant Jewish artefacts such as a prayer shawl, kippah or menorah?

Bar mitzvah quiz

The aim of this gap-fill activity is to reinforce some of the vocabulary relating to the topic and to assess understanding. Before filling in the gaps on the whiteboard, ask everyone to copy out the words, leaving the gaps. Alternatively, you can print out the page. Pupils should then fill in the gaps on their copies.

After they have completed it themselves, invite suggestions for dragging words to fill the gaps in the six sentences on the whiteboard. NB Some of the words are decoys.

To encourage empathy and personal responses, ask the class to imagine that they were a guest at either Jonathan's bar mitzvah or Tanya's bat mitzvah and to write a card or letter saying what happened and why it was special for Jonathan or Tanya.

Christianity

A Roman Catholic First Communion

Roman Catholic churches usually hold a special service called First Communion when children are 7 years old. Following this, they can receive Holy Communion at Mass. The teaching of the Roman Catholic Church is that there are three Sacraments of Initiation: Baptism, Confirmation and the Eucharist (or Mass or Holy Communion). In most Roman Catholic dioceses in the UK, confirmation happens after receiving Communion, but in some areas young people do not receive Communion until after they have been confirmed.

A similar diversity of practice happens in the Church of England/Anglican Church, where normal practice has been not to admit someone to Communion before he or she has been confirmed. However, more Anglican dioceses are now admitting children to Communion before confirmation.

It is commonly thought that, while the baptism of an infant welcomes the child into the Church, First Communion happens when a person is old enough (usually 7 years old) to appreciate that he or she belongs to the Church family. At confirmation, often years later, he or she affirms for him or herself a commitment to the beliefs into which he or she was baptised years before.

Discuss all the features of the video that suggest this is a very special occasion. Some children may be confused that the girls are in what appear to be bridal dresses and the boys in page outfits. The symbolism represents their being committed to Jesus Christ, resolved to live pure lives and to avoid doing wrong.

You may wish to do the activity described on page 3 of the notepad: to draw a wall display made up of interlocking circles, based around each person in the class. The circles represent all the different groups and activities to which the pupils belong. These might include the family, the school, the church or other religious group, the swimming club, and so on.

A Church of England confirmation service

Confirmation is the service in both the Roman Catholic and Anglican Church when young people and adults confirm in public the vows made, often on their behalf when they were babies, to follow Jesus Christ and to renounce evil. The confirmation service shown in this slideshow was held in a Church of England parish church in London.

In the audio commentary, some young people describe the time when they were confirmed. After listening to them, ask the class what seems to stand out as being special and important about the service.

If you wish to look more closely at an image, it can be frozen and enlarged while you explore the content.

As with bar and bat mitzvah in Judaism, confirmation admits someone into full membership of the Church. Because of the importance of this and to lend significance, the service is presided over by a bishop. Not only does the candidate 'confirm' his or her faith, but the bishop prays for God to 'confirm' or assure him or her of God's love and presence.

This is an extract from the confirmation service of the Church of England:

Confirmation

Bishop:

Our help is in the name of the Lord, who has made heaven and earth.

Blessed be the name of the Lord, now and for ever. Amen.

Almighty and ever-living God,

you have given these your servants new birth in baptism by water and the Spirit,

and have forgiven them all their sins.

Let your Holy Spirit rest upon them:

the Spirit of wisdom and understanding;

the Spirit of counsel and inward strength;

the Spirit of knowledge and true godliness;

and let their delight be in the fear of the Lord. Amen.

The candidates come forward. Godparents and parents/family/friends may stand when their son/daughter is named.

The bishop addresses each candidate by name:

XXX, God has called you by name and made you his own.

He then lays his hand on the head of each, saying:

Confirm, O Lord, your servant with your Holy Spirit. Amen

All:

Defend, O Lord, these your servants with your heavenly grace,

that they may continue yours for ever,

and daily increase in your Holy Spirit more and more until

they come to your everlasting kingdom. Amen.

Confirmation quiz

This is a quiz about confirmation in the Church of England. The gap-fill activity is designed to consolidate the vocabulary learned from the previous page. NB Some words are decoys.

Baptism in the river Jordan

Many Christians choose to be baptised as adults. Amongst these, some are baptised by 'total immersion'. As with other forms of baptism, water is the key symbolic element, as the candidates believe that through faith in Jesus, their sins are forgiven or 'washed away'. Baptism is an outward sign of this. In addition, many who are baptised by immersion also see it as representing death and resurrection – in going down into the water and then rising from it they believe they are showing that they are 'dying' to the past and 'rising' to new life. It is a public declaration that they are committing themselves to be followers of Jesus, i.e. Christians.

Most Christians who choose to be baptised by immersion do so at a local church. (See the next page, *Baptism in a Baptist church*, for an example of this.) For those who travel to the river Jordan for their baptism, there is special significance in being baptised in the river where Jesus himself was baptised. One account of this can be found in St Matthew's Gospel, chapter 3, verses 13-17.

Jesus was baptised by his cousin, John. This was not a Christian rite, but a Jewish one, relating to Jewish ritual cleansing from sin. By being baptised, Jesus was identifying with John's call to Jews to commit themselves afresh to living by the principles of the Torah, or God's Law. For Christians, the narratives of Jesus' baptism make it clear that this is one of the first declarations that he was the Son of God.

Talk about why, for some Christians, being baptised in the river Jordan is a very special occasion.

Baptism in a Baptist church

Baptist churches, together with a few others such as the Pentecostal denominations, do not baptise infants. They believe that people should wait until they are old enough to understand the meaning of it for themselves. It is sometimes known as 'Believers' Baptism'. All Baptist churches have a baptistery (or baptistry) built into the floor of the main worship area. This is a water tank in which the person to be baptised and the minister stand. Usually, the candidate speaks, as a public witness, about his or her faith in Jesus, after which he or she is baptised by total immersion. Family and friends usually attend and, for everyone present, it is a very moving occasion.

Look at the picture shown at marker 1 before watching the video. What do the pupils think is happening? Discuss the reasons for being baptised, whether by immersion or not. How can you tell that this occasion means a great deal to the person being baptised in the video?

In churches where baptism by immersion is not generally practised, young people and adults are usually baptised in the same way as infants – with water symbolically poured onto the head at a font. If someone in, say, an Anglican church wishes to be baptised by immersion, sometimes a tank is hired and brought into the church, sometimes a Baptist church is used or it may take place in a swimming pool.

Sikhism

The story of the Khalsa

A key rite of passage for Sikhs is when, as young people or adults, they join the Khalsa, the grouping to which all committed Sikhs belong. This video tells the story of the founding of the Khalsa by Guru Gobind Singh, the final great Sikh leader, or Guru, who lived from 1666 to 1708.

He devised a test to discover a group of Sikhs whose commitment would be exceptional. They had to be prepared to die for their beliefs.

The five men who volunteered were called the Panj Pyare, or 'Beloved ones'. They were drawn from all Indian castes or classes and this demonstrates the Sikh belief in the equality of all.

People have different views about what happened after the brave volunteers went into the Guru's tent. Was their 'death', from which they apparently recovered, a pretence devised for the challenge, or did they die and then miraculously revive again? Whatever happened, the event became a benchmark of commitment for all Sikhs.

Taking amrit

Nowadays, Sikhs express their commitment to Sikhism by being initiated in the Khalsa in a ceremony that involves taking a drink called amrit, which is made of sugar and water. Often this is done at the festival of Baisakhi, when the main focus is the Khalsa. The ceremony is presided over by five men who, in recollection of Guru Gobind Singh's original five devotees, are called the Panj Pyare. They dress in splendid clothes that make them stand out from all other Sikhs on the day. They carry ceremonial swords with which they prayerfully mix the sugar and water of the amrit.

This video shows extremely rare footage of Sikhs taking amrit. Generally, it is conducted behind closed doors with only the Panj Pyare and the initiates present. This is because it is seen as a sacred and intimate moment in a Sikh's life.

At the ceremony, Sikh men and women make solemn vows to live by the principles of Sikhism, as taught by the Gurus and expressed in their holy book, the Guru Granth Sahib. This is a life of devotion to God and moral goodness. They also commit themselves to wearing the Five Ks, which are featured on the next page, *The Five Ks*.

Striking video sequences of the festival of Baisakhi can be found in *Whiteboard Active: Celebrations and Special Times* (BBC Active, 2007).

The Five Ks

The Five Ks are symbols that remind Sikhs constantly of the commitment they made in taking amrit. The turban, probably the most distinctive and visible item of clothing associated with Sikh men, is not one of the five Ks. It is linked, however, to one of the Ks: the long, uncut hair, known as *kesh*. The turban is a means of keeping the uncut hair tidy.

The five Ks are:

Kesh – uncut hair

Khanga – a small comb with which the long hair is kept in place

Kara – a bracelet, representing the unending, eternal nature of God

Kaccha – shorts worn as an undergarment as a symbol of purity

Kirpan – a small ornamental dagger, representing the willingness to stand up for one's beliefs

In addition to exploring the meaning of the Five Ks, this video provides an opportunity to look at symbols in general and, in particular, the use of symbols in a variety of religions.

Five Ks quiz

The aim of this drag-and-drop labelling activity is to consolidate the knowledge and understanding of the Five Ks. It is suggested that pupils work out the answers on their own before completing the activity on the whiteboard. You may wish to print off the page for each person or group.

Writing focus: A special time in my life

This encourages thought and reflection about any special time in the children's lives. They are invited to write about a time which they consider important, to explain why it was significant and what happened.

A world of weddings

The eight photographs in this slideshow are of wedding ceremonies around the world: Peru, Greece, Tanzania, Ethiopia, Sri Lanka, Bali, Japan and Fiji. You may wish to locate the countries on a world map or globe.

The images offer the opportunity to discuss the similarities between marriage ceremonies everywhere and why in all communities this is regarded as one of the most important moments in people's lives.

Discuss with the class what happens at religious and non-religious weddings in the UK. Look in a local paper, finding out from the photographs and reports what appear to be the common features of weddings in your area.

Talk about a marriage ceremony being significant on several levels:

- for the couple who are getting married
- for their families who are becoming linked with a new person and his or her family
- for the friends who, with the families, witness the wedding as part of the community
- for fulfilling the legal requirements, so that a couple is married in accordance with the law of the country
- in the case of a religious ceremony, for God, who is seen as blessing the couple's union.

Choosing a partner

This drag-and-drop activity provides a springboard for discussing how people choose their partners. The class is invited to consider eight comments from children about the characteristics that they would like to see in a partner. They are invited to put them in their preferred order. There are no right or wrong answers. It is suggested that they do this individually and then the class votes on which they would put at the top and bottom of the list, before doing the activity on the whiteboard.

Are there any characteristics that they would like to add to the list?

Talk about being single. Many people remain single by choice and/or circumstances. Are there advantages to being single? Discuss the vows that Roman Catholic priests and nuns make to remain single, devoted to Jesus and to serving God and other people.

Christianity

A Christian wedding

This video shows a traditional church wedding – in this case, in a Church of England parish church. The service has both religious and legal dimensions. During the service, it is made clear that the ceremony is being conducted 'in the sight of God' and that, by opting for a church service, the wedding couple acknowledge that their new union is not just a matter for the two of them or for the two of them and their families and friends: it is at its heart a union sealed by vows made to one another in the presence of God.

This union is symbolised by the giving and receiving of rings. The unbroken circle of the ring represents both the unending love of the couple for one another and also God's eternal nature and love for all people.

The service is conducted by the priest, usually the vicar or rector of the local parish with which the bride or groom has links.

Many of the 'traditional' features associated with weddings are not historically very old. For example, in earlier centuries the bride and groom met in the porch, where the civil ceremony was held, before they walked into the church together for the religious ceremony.

A key element is the union of two families, through the couple. It is a long-standing tradition for the bride's father to 'give away' his daughter formally to the bridegroom as part of the service, although now in some churches, when asked the question, 'Who gives this woman to be married to this man?' both the bride's parents say, 'We do.' The congregation is now often invited to promise to support the couple in their new life together.

Some clergy have conducted simulated weddings in a church or in school, with children playing the parts of all the people involved and using an edited form of service. If a local priest or minister is willing to do this, it can be a rewarding project, especially if thought is given to all aspects of the preparation.

Marriage vows

This home video gives an opportunity to look closely at the marriage vows, the central part of the wedding service. Before showing this sequence, ask the class to think about the way the couple are saying the vows. What impression do they get of what the couple are thinking and feeling?

These are the vows used in the video by James and Alexa-Maria. They are from the Church of England Marriage Service:

I, James/Alexa-Maria, take you, Alexa-Maria/James, to be my wife/husband: to have and to hold, from this day forward; for better, for worse; for richer, for poorer; in sickness and in health; to love and to cherish, till death us do part, according to God's holy law. In the presence of God I make this vow.

Talk about why the word 'vow' is used rather than 'promise': this is to give extra weight or seriousness to the words.

Ask the class to imagine that they were getting married. What promises would they like their new partner to make in addition to those already included in the wedding ceremony?

This video, like the previous one, offers useful images of church interiors that could be used when doing work on places of worship. This is also the case for other sections of this CD-ROM.

Jesus goes to a wedding

In the Church of England wedding service, reference is made to an occasion when Jesus was at a wedding. The account can be found in St John's Gospel, chapter 2, verses 1 to 11. It took place at Cana, a village in the Galilean hills, not far from Jesus' home town of Nazareth. It is mentioned in services to show that Jesus honoured marriage, even though he himself never married. It was at this wedding that, according to the New Testament, Jesus' first miracle took place. In it he changed water to wine, when there was no wine left, in order to save the host from embarrassment. It was one of the early incidents that established Jesus' religious authority. The account says that 'he revealed his glory in this way and his disciples put their faith in him'.

Jesus also demonstrated that he understood the importance of a wedding being a good celebratory party. Talk about this aspect of weddings. If pupils have been to a wedding, they will be able to talk about the reception that followed the marriage ceremony.

Most rites of passage have a strong community element associated with them. The community, represented by families and friends, is present at the marriage itself and then, afterwards, in the party-like reception, the community celebrates the couple's new married life together.

Judaism

A Jewish wedding

The video shows a Jewish wedding in a synagogue. It is not essential for Jewish couples to be married in a synagogue. Wherever it takes place, the couple and the rabbi usually stand under a flower-decorated canopy called a *huppah* or *chuppah*. (There are varied spellings of the word, as they are transliterations from Hebrew.) The *huppah* symbolises the hope that the couple will remain under God's blessing and protection for ever; it also represents the home they will share.

Jewish weddings can be held on any day of the week except during the Sabbath or on High Holy Days such as Rosh Hashanah or Yom Kippur.

In the week before the marriage, a ceremony known as Ufruf is arranged for the groom: he goes to the synagogue, takes part in the service and announces the wedding. The bride will often visit the ritual bath, known as the Mikveh, so that she can cleanse herself spiritually.

Seven cups of wine are drunk during and after the ceremony, echoing the seven days of the Genesis Creation story.

Rings have a similar symbolism as in a Christian marriage. As the bridegroom gives the ring to the bride, he says, 'Behold, you are consecrated to me with this ring, according to the laws of Moses and Israel.'

Prayers or blessings are said by the rabbi for the couple in their new life together.

The ceremony ends with the breaking of a glass by the groom, as shown in the video. This recollects the destruction of the Temple in Jerusalem many centuries ago, so that the couple will know that God's blessing is upon them when times are hard, as much as when they are good.

At the reception, in Orthodox communities, men and women dance separately. Among the religious customs observed at the reception, blessings are said over challah bread and seven blessings are made for the bride and groom.

The story of Ruth and Boaz

This is an audio-visual retelling of a great Jewish story of love and devotion. It is part of the Hebrew Bible, known to Christians as the Old Testament. A complete book, entitled 'The Book of Ruth', is given over to telling Ruth's story.

Because of poor harvests, a family from Bethlehem travelled to the land of Moab to survive. They were Elimelech, his wife Naomi and their two sons, Mahlon and Kilion. In Moab, the sons met and married two Moabite women named Ruth and Orpah. Ten years after Elimelech died, the two sons died, leaving the three women: Naomi, Ruth and Orpah. Things were difficult for them, so Naomi decided to return to Bethlehem where the harvests were plentiful again. Naomi gave Ruth and Orpah the chance to stay in Moab. Orpah did this, but Ruth opted to travel with Naomi and to care for her, even though she knew no one in Bethlehem. In these celebrated words, Ruth expressed her commitment: 'Where you will go, I will go. Where you stay, I will stay. Your people will be my people and your God will be my God.' Her commitment illustrates the new bonds that come about through marriage.

When Naomi and Ruth reached Bethlehem, they are looked after by a land-owning relative named Boaz. Eventually, Ruth and Boaz married. Among their descendants was David, who became the most famous king of Israel.

Talk about the theme of self-sacrifice. How much did Ruth give up by leaving Moab? What made her give up so much?

Hinduism

A Hindu wedding

A Hindu couple reflect on their marriage as they look at a family film. They describe how they had an arranged marriage. In their case, this meant that their parents introduced them to several prospective partners, from whom they chose the person they wished to marry.

There are many variations in Hindu wedding ceremonies. In a typical one, the bridegroom arrives at the ceremony to be welcomed by the bride's family and garlanded by the bride. There is a 'handing over' moment, when the bride's father entrusts her to the groom's safe-keeping: this may involve the father placing his daughter's hand in the groom's hand. Sometimes a hymn is recited by the groom, asking for the blessing of love. The bride and groom often wear clothing in whites and reds, to represent fidelity, wealth and purity. The bride's hands and feet will probably have been painted with elaborate henna patterns.

The priest ties the bride's veil to the groom's scarf, and then rings and garlands are exchanged.

Central to the ceremony is the marriage fire or flame. It represents the divine presence (Agni) who is seen as a divine witness to the union. A key moment happens when bride and groom walk around the fire seven times, linked by the ties scarf and veil. In some communities, it is only four times. As the couple walk round the fire, they may make offerings into the fire and pray for wealth, good fortune and fidelity. In India, this is generally seen as the moment when the marriage has become legalised. After this, the couple may stand on a stone to symbolise their prayer that their love should be on a solid foundation of love.

The ritual of the Seven Steps often happens. In this, the bride and groom together take seven steps, not necessarily round the fire, asking for a blessing at each step. They pray for nourishment, strength, prosperity, happiness, the gift of children, long life and devoted union.

Much of the ceremony is conducted by a priest in the ancient language of Sanskrit. As few people today understand Sanskrit, there will also be parts in the local language of the people.

The story of Rama and Sita

Hindus see Rama and Sita as role models for a devoted, loving couple and try to live up to their example. Some Hindu marriage ceremonies refer to them as examples to be followed.

The story, from the Ramayana, an ancient narrative, is well known: Sita is enticed away from her husband, Rama, by the evil Ravana. She is taken as a prisoner to the island of Lanka, from which, after a fierce battle, she is rescued by Rama and Hanuman, the Monkey King, and reunited with Rama. They return to their kingdom, with celebratory lamps lighting their way home.

Frequently, some of the names of characters in the story are written without a final letter 'a'. For example, Ram (pronounced to rhyme with 'arm'), Ravan and Ramayan.

The story is retold in many different ways, including puppetry. Find a way of retelling the story, perhaps using masks to represent the characters.

Writing focus: A letter about a wedding

This page should be viewed after watching all the videos in this unit. It is suggested that the class imagine that they have been at one of the weddings shown in the videos. They write to a friend explaining what happened and their feelings about the occasion.

Unit 5: The end of the journey

The end of this life's journey

This unit provides pupils with an opportunity to share their feelings of loss caused by separation and to learn about how faith can provide believers with answers to life's most challenging and ultimate questions and the rituals that help people to mark the loss of a loved one.

The aim of this introduction is to encourage pupils to consider the view that death is a natural part of life and not something to be unnecessarily anxious about. The question 'What happens when someone dies?' has been asked by successive generations of people and the answers that have been given vary from age to age and faith to faith. This introduction raises awareness of a variety of answers, pointing out that, although religious views on the afterlife vary, religious people believe that something of a human being – the spirit, *atman* or soul – can survive in some form after the human body has died.

This introduction also emphasises that the human experience of grief is a normal expression of loss, whether a person is a believer or not. Teachers need to be aware that pupils from strongly religious backgrounds may feel that their faith is not good enough if they feel these human feelings. They will need to be reassured that all humans feel grief whether they believe or not – it is a normal part of human expression of feeling and a natural outcome of relationships with others.

Many pupils will find it easier to approach this topic by distancing it to the experiences of others – so, considering how to help someone else is a way for pupils who have experienced grief to share feelings and views based on the experience of others.

Hinduism

What do Hindus believe about the journey of life?

Hindus believe that death is the not end of life; it is the start of a new life. They believe that this life is just one of many that a soul, or *atman*, will experience, learning new lessons each time.

Hinduism teaches that any attempt to find permanent happiness in this world is *maya* (an illusion). They believe that a person's spirit, or *atman*, is permanent and cannot change while the physical body is not permanent and can change. The *atman* is reborn many times – *samsara*, or reincarnation. If pupils are old or able enough, you might like to introduce this quotation from the Hindu holy text the Bhagavad Gita:

'As a man casts off his worn-out clothes and takes on other new ones, so does the embodied soul cast off his worn-out bodies and enters other new.'

The journey of a soul in reincarnation can be described as like a candle being lit from the flame of another that is guttering and dying – not as a consciousness being transferred from one body to another.

Beliefs about reincarnation are also held by Sikhs and Buddhists, and these like many other faiths favour cremation. Hindu mourners are encouraged to chant prayers without excessive displays of grief to help the departed soul to detach its feelings and emotions from the family members it leaves behind and to move on in its journey. Hindu priests emphasise the route ahead for the departed soul and a funeral is as much a celebration as a remembrance service.

Rajiv Gandhi's funeral

In India, Hindus hope to have their funeral at the burning ghats on the shores of the sacred river Ganges, where the body is placed on a large pile of wood and the eldest son says the appropriate Vedic prayers and lights the fire. Incense and ghee are poured into the flames.

This state funeral shows these very personal last offices a family does for the departed relative. Here you see Rajiv Gandhi's wife and children helping to fuel the pyre and light it. The funeral is conducted by a Brahmin priest and Rajiv Gandhi's son says prayers and lights the funeral fire in the video. Family members and mourners offer their respects and final farewells by circumambulating the body once and placing flowers at the feet of the departed.

In the United Kingdom, Hindu funerals do not take place on a funeral pyre in the open, although in some parts of the UK the Hindu and Sikh community are trying to get local councils to work towards this. In the UK, the deceased is placed in a coffin that will be taken to a crematorium.

Whether in India or the UK, after a cremation the ashes of the dead person are usually sprinkled on water. Many Hindus take the ashes to India to put on the waters of the Ganges, others may take them to the sea near to where they live.

During and after the funeral, the widow or widower will wear white as a sign of mourning, as seen in this video. Formal mourning lasts for twelve days.

Buddhism

Prince Siddartha's search for meaning

This slideshow explores the life of Prince Siddartha and his journey to find the answer to the questions of why there is suffering in the world.

The Buddha taught the four Noble Truths:

- Life involves suffering.
- The origins of suffering lie in wanting, which is made more intense by greed, hatred and ignorance.
- The ending of suffering is possible.
- Following the Noble Eightfold Path is the way to end suffering and become enlightened.

Buddhists believe that when people die, they are reborn as another kind of being – not always as a human. The Buddha taught that all things change and pass away; including everyone and everything we love. He also taught that whatever kind of being we are now (e.g. a human or an animal), we won't stay like this in every life. Each life may be short or long, happy or unhappy, but the one thing we all have in common is that we will die at some point. After that we will be reborn as another being, maybe a completely different kind of being. This is why Buddhists teach that everyone should always try to be kind to other living things because we are all connected like members of one great universal family.

The endless cycle of the birth and death is called *samsara*, which means something like 'continually moving on'. All beings are trapped in *samsara*.

Buddhists believe that the things we do and the way we think are important in this life and that they affect the kind of rebirth that we will have. This is the idea of karma, which means 'action'. In Buddhism, it matters how we behave. The way we act now shapes our present life, and our actions also have a powerful influence on the kind of being we become after we die and are reborn.

The story of Kisa and the mustard seeds

The story of Kisa and the mustard seeds shows how the Buddha found a clever way of showing the grieving mother that death comes to everyone by asking her to get some mustard seeds from a house where nobody has ever died. This allows Kisa to discover for herself the truth that everyone dies and nothing lasts forever. She can then accept the death of her child and begin to grieve. In order to make sure that pupils appreciate the commonality of mustard seeds in the locality where the story takes place, it might help to discuss what you might find in every home around the school – salt, for example.

Then they will appreciate why the request appeared so simple to Kisa at the outset, but also how framing the request in this way ensured Kisa would not be able to fulfil the Buddha's request, therefore leading her to find the answer to her situation through her own experience.

Christianity

What do Christians believe Easter tells them about life's end?

The two most important aspects of Easter are the death and the resurrection of Jesus, who Christians believe to be the Son of God. Through Jesus' death they believe that they can experience God's loving forgiveness and acceptance, both in this life and after death for ever. Belief in the resurrection of Jesus assures them that death is not the end of existence, but that life continues, albeit in a different, spiritual form. The resurrection offers them the hope that God will be with them now and that they will be together with God after death. The celebration of Easter is therefore at the heart of Christian belief and experience.

What do Christians believe happens when someone dies?

Christians believe that death is not an end. They believe that, if life after death is spent with God, then that will be a wonderful time, with no more pain or suffering. They have hope in this new life because they believe that Jesus rose from the dead after he had been crucified. Our physical bodies come to an end at death. However, Christians believe that, after death, life continues in a new sort of spiritual life in which a person's essence or essential nature is still identifiable.

In the video, David tells the story of the water bugs and dragonflies to explain how he feels his dead sister was transformed after her death and has a life somewhere that she is not able to share with him while he is still on earth.

The story helps him to make sense of the separation he has experienced and yet the closeness that his faith leads him to believe they can still experience.

The story is linked to the theme of new life at Easter. Here, the Greek Orthodox tradition of preparing and cracking coloured eggs is seen – eggs are a symbol of Easter in many parts of the Christian church in many countries. Eggs are pre-Christian symbols of new life.

Christianity incorporated them into Easter celebrations to reflect the new life of Jesus. New life, in the form of a chick, hatches from the stillness of an egg. This, for Christians, symbolises Jesus emerging to new life from the stillness of the tomb. You may wish to discuss the Christian ideas of new life: the belief that Jesus can make a difference to their lives, giving a new quality of life, and that this life continues after death.

A place of rest

Graveyards and cemeteries are places of remembrance and memories. This video encourages pupils to develop appreciation of this, as well as sensitivity to people who may visit them to remember loved ones through quiet thought or tending a grave.

The graves in this graveyard are Christian graves, although Muslims and Jews believe in burying their loved ones too.

On the gravestones you can see the names of the people who are buried, as well as the dates of the years in which they were born and died. There are sometimes messages too that show how much they have meant to their families and friends.

If there is a graveyard near your school, you may like to go to investigate what it teaches about the locality and local people. For example, local surnames may feature that show how families have been associated with the area for a long time. Times when a large number of deaths occurred may indicate illness, epidemics or terrible accidents in the locality.

Parents/carers should be clear about what any visit will involve and should be encouraged to inform the school if they have anxieties or concerns as early as possible. This will enable steps to be taken to allay these concerns and reassure them that their child is being supported with great care. For example, parents/carers may be concerned for the welfare of any pupil who has recently suffered bereavement or is going through a grieving process.

Provision is made in the literacy hour in England at Key Stage 2 for epitaphs to be explored and a visit to a graveyard can provide pupils with first-hand examples to discuss back at school. However, care needs to be taken when selecting epitaphs to study and considering how to use them in lessons. Epitaphs come in many forms and styles, ranging from comic to profound. These different expressions need to be explored, along with the reasons why the writer has selected a particular style. Pupils could think they give the message that life is cheap and people who die are not missed – not the message anyone would like to give.

A graveyard with a difference

This graveyard visited by Michael Palin in Romania differs from traditional graveyards in the UK by its cheerful, sometimes irreverent images on the tombs. However, the paintings do tell the visitor something about the life and personality of the dead people buried there. Pupils from certain Christian denominations will know of the tradition of showing a picture of the deceased in some graveyards, so this colourful scene will be less incongruous to them. Those who have studied the ancient Egyptians will know the value placed on the decoration of a sarcophagus throughout the Egyptian dynasties, some of the latter of which included images of the deceased painted on the outer coffin.

What do pupils think of graveyards that might tell more about the people buried there? Do they feel these places are less serious, or would you be more likely to remember the lives of those who have died?

Going to a Christian funeral

When a Christian dies, it is seen as the end of his or her life on earth. A funeral is held for friends and family to grieve for the person who has died and give thanks for his or her life. The funeral is held about a week after death. It can take place in a church or at a crematorium, as many Christians do not have particular religious views about which is preferable. This funeral is a burial in a graveyard, similar to that seen in the previous video, *A place of rest*.

The Helen House hospice was developed after Sister Frances Dominica supported the parents of a seriously ill little girl called Helen who lived at home with her family and required 24-hour care. Helen's family's experience highlighted the need for respite care and support for the families of children with life-shortening conditions. Helen House was set up to help families cope by providing occasional respite care tailored to individual needs.

A children's hospice is unlikely to be suitable for someone who is 16 or over, but neither is an adult hospice, which is why Douglas House was opened in February 2004. It is a place where very ill young adults aged 16 to about 35 can experience life in a positive setting.

Older or more able pupils might like to research the hospice movement and, if there is a hospice in your area, you might like to invite someone in to the class to talk about how they support the patients and their families. Alternatively, a Christian minister or funeral director might be a useful visitor to talk about how funerals can be planned to ensure they are also an opportunity to celebrate the life of the deceased.

Marking an end and celebrating a life

This video shows footage of the Christian state funeral of Queen Elizabeth the Queen Mother. She was over a hundred years old when she died. A state funeral is a public funeral ceremony held to honour heads of state or other important people of national significance. Having such a public event televised let millions of people who had admired her life share in the service.

During a state funeral there is a time when the body is lying in state before the funeral service, usually at Westminster Abbey. During the lying in state, the coffin rests on a catafalque in the middle of Westminster Hall and members of the public are able to file past to show their respects. Each corner of the coffin is guarded by various units of the Sovereign's Bodyguard or the Household Division. However, during the funeral of both King George V and Queen Elizabeth the Queen Mother, male members of the Royal Family mounted the guard in what has become known as the Vigil of the Princes. For George V, his four sons – King Edward VIII, the Duke of York, the Duke of Gloucester and the Duke of Kent – stood guard. For the Queen Mother, her grandsons – the Prince of Wales, the Duke of York, the Earl of Wessex and Viscount Linley – took these positions, as seen in the video.

Helping us to remember

This video shows how a class brought in to their school a range of items that helped them to remember people who had died and who were very special to them. It shows how the memories unlocked are vivid and meaningful. You may wish to replicate this activity for your class, helping them to celebrate the lives of those who meant so much to them.

Before watching the video or engaging in this activity, you may like to discuss with the class what it is that makes something meaningful and special and to draw up a code of conduct for treating things that are special to others with care and respect.

Writing focus: My life journey

What would I like my life journey to achieve? This task provides an opportunity for pupils to consider life's potential, and to affirm personal goals and aims.

Curriculum grid

Unit 1: Introduction

Page	Learning objective	QCA link
The journey of life	To encourage a range of responses to images of important events in people's lives	Themes: h Experiences and opportunities: p
Growing old	To stimulate thought and discussion about ageing and experiencing different stages in life	Themes: h Experience and opportunities: p
What makes people happy?	To understand that happiness means different things to different people and to consider the factors that lead to contentment	Themes: h Experience and opportunities: p

Unit 2: Birth

Page	Learning objective	QCA link
The start of life	To appreciate the preparations and experiences leading up to the birth of a baby To consider the extended family and community that share the joy of the birth of a baby	Learning about religion: a Learning from religion: a Themes: h Experiences and opportunities: p
Islam The birth of a baby is a blessing	To know that Muslims celebrate the gift of a baby by sharing with those less fortunate	Learning about religion: a, b, e Learning from religion: a, b Themes: h, i, k Experiences and opportunities: p
What's in a name?	To understand how names express uniqueness and also belonging To consider how the choice of name can link to people who are special to our family	Learning about religion: b Themes: j Experiences and opportunities: p
Sikhism Choosing a name	To know Sikh beliefs and customs about choosing a name for a baby To understand the central significance of the Guru Granth Sahib in daily and family life	Learning about religion: a, b, e Learning from religion: a, b, c Themes: e, g, h, i, k Experiences and opportunities: p
Christianity A Christian Baptism	To know how a Church of England baptism welcomes a baby into the family of the church To know and understand some of the elements of a baptism service To consider the feelings of those involved in the service	Learning about religion: a, b Learning from religion: a, b Themes: e, h, i, k, l Experiences and opportunities: p, q
Writing focus: A big responsibility	To consider the issues that influence Christian parents when choosing the godparents for a new baby To reflect on the qualities needed for a good godparent	Learning about religion: a Learning from religion: a, b Themes: e, h Experiences and opportunities: p
Welcome to the Christian family	To know that welcoming a baby into the Christian family may vary in different parts of the church To recognise similarities between a dedication service and an infant baptism service	Learning about religion: a, b, e Learning from religion: a, Themes: g, h, k, l Experiences and opportunities: p, q
A welcome for Jesus	To know the story of Jesus' dedication service at the Temple To understand the significance for Christians that Simeon and Anna recognised the baby as the one they had been waiting for	Learning about religion: a, b, c Learning from religion: a, b Themes: e Experiences and opportunities: p

Unit 3: Growing up

Page	Learning objective	QCA link
Changes and new beginnings	To consider the likely thoughts and emotions which can accompany major changes, such as moving to secondary school	Experiences and opportunities: p
Judaism Bar mitzvah	To know that a bar mitzvah marks the coming of age for a Jewish boy and to understand its importance	Learning about religion: a, b, e Learning from religion: a, b Themes: e, g, h Experiences and opportunities: p, q
Bar mitzvah and bat mitzvah ceremonies	To appreciate how Jewish boys and girls feel before and during their bar or bat mitzvah	Learning about religion: a, b, e Learning from religion: a, b Themes: e, g, h Experiences and opportunities: p, q
Bar mitzvah quiz	To consolidate knowledge of vocabulary relating to bar mitzvah	Learning about religion: a, b, e Learning from religion: a, b Themes: e, g, h Experiences and opportunities: p, q
Christianity A Roman Catholic First Communion	To learn about what it means to take your First Communion and how the service shows its importance	Learning about religion: a, b, e Learning from religion: a, b, e Themes: e, g, h Experiences and opportunities: p, q
A Church of England confirmation service	To understand that at confirmation a person 'confirms' the vows made at baptism	Learning about religion: a, b, c Learning from religion: a, b Themes: e, g, h, i Experiences and opportunities: p, q
Confirmation quiz	To consolidate knowledge of vocabulary relating to confirmation	Learning about religion: a, b Learning from religion: a, b Themes: e, g, h, i Experiences and opportunities: p
Baptism in the river Jordan	To find out about baptism by total immersion and about the baptism of Jesus	Learning about religion: a, b, c Learning from religion: a, b Themes: e, g, h, i Experiences and opportunities: p, q
Baptism in a Baptist church	To understand the importance and meaning of adult baptism by immersion in the Baptist tradition	Learning about religion: a, b, c Learning from religion: a, b Themes: e, g, h, i Experiences and opportunities: p, q
Sikhism The story of the Khalsa	To learn about Guru Gobind Singh and the beginnings of the Khalsa	Learning about religion: a, b, c Learning from religion: a, b Themes: e, g, h, i, j Experiences and opportunities: p, q
Taking amrit	To consider the meaning of commitment and to understand the significance of taking amrit	Learning about religion: a, b, e Learning from religion: a, b, c Themes: e, g, h, i, j Experiences and opportunities: p, q
The Five Ks	To learn what the Five Ks are and what they symbolise	Learning about religion: a, b, c, e, g Learning from religion: a, b, c Themes: e, g, h, i Experiences and opportunities: p, q
Five Ks quiz	To consolidate knowledge of vocabulary relating to the Five Ks	Learning about religion: g
Writing focus: A special time in my life	To encourage reflection and response about important moments in life	Learning from religion: c

Unit 4: Marriage

Page	Learning objective	QCA link
A world of weddings	To appreciate that marriage is a worldwide institution with similarities and differences	Learning about religion: b, e Learning from religion: a, b, c Themes: e, g, h, i, k Experiences and opportunities: p
Choosing a partner	To consider the characteristics of a good life partner and how people make choices	Learning about religion: a, b Learning from religion: a, b, d Themes: e, g, h, i, j, k Experiences and opportunities: p, q
Christianity A Christian wedding	To learn about what happens in many traditional church weddings and the importance for individuals, the community and the church	Learning about religion: a, b, e Learning from religion: a, b Themes: e, g, h, i, k, l Experiences and opportunities: p, q
Marriage vows	To understand the importance of the vows in a marriage service	Learning about religion: a, b, e Learning from religion: a, b Themes: e, g, h, i, k, l Experiences and opportunities: p, q
Jesus goes to a wedding	To learn what happens in the New Testament narrative of this occasion and to understand that it would have been a Jewish wedding	Learning about religion: a, e Learning from religion: a Themes: e, f, g, h, i, j Experiences and opportunities: p
Judaism A Jewish wedding	To find out about some features of a Jewish wedding and some similarities with weddings shown in earlier pages	Learning about religion: a, b, e Learning from religion: a, b Themes: e, g, h, i, k, l Experiences and opportunities: p, q
The story of Ruth and Boaz	To become familiar with the story and the reasons why Ruth became a role model of commitment to others	Learning about religion: a Learning from religion: c Themes: e, f, h, j Experiences and opportunities: p, q
Hinduism A Hindu wedding	To learn about some aspects of a Hindu marriage	Learning about religion: a, b, e Learning from religion: a, b Themes: e, g, h, i, k, l Experiences and opportunities: p, q
The story of Rama and Sita	To learn about the story and how it provides an example of commitment and love	Learning about religion: a Learning from religion: c Themes: e, f, h, j Experiences and opportunities: p, q
Writing focus: A letter about a wedding	Using observation and empathy, to reflect on the importance of marriage ceremonies in many people's lives	Learning from religion: c Themes: h Experiences and opportunities: p

Unit 5: The end of the journey

Page	Learning objective	QCA link
The end of this life's journey	To reflect on how life and death are part of one journey To introduce reflection on and empathy towards feelings of grief and loss - natural responses to death	Learning about religion: a, b, c Learning from religion: a, b Themes: e Experiences and opportunities: p
Hinduism What do Hindus believe about the journey of life?	To know Hindu beliefs about the cycle of life – death and rebirth To understand how Hindus believe cremation helps the spirit to its next rebirth	Learning about religion: a, b Learning from religion: a, b, c Themes: e, h, i Experiences and opportunities: p, q
Rajiv Gandhi's funeral	To know how a Hindu cremation is organised To appreciate that believers experience grief and sadness	Learning about religion: a, b, d, e Learning from religion: a, b Themes: e, k, m Experiences and opportunities: p
Buddhism Prince Siddartha's search for meaning	To know that suffering in all its forms inspired the Buddha's search for meaning and purpose in life	Learning about religion: a, e, f Learning from religion: c, e Themes: f, h, j Experiences and opportunities: p, q
The story of Kisa and the mustard seeds	To know and understand the Buddha's teaching that death is an inevitable part of life	Learning about religion: a, c, f Learning from religion: c Themes: e, f, h Experiences and opportunities: p, q
Christianity What do Christians believe Easter tells them about life's end?	To understand the connection that Christians make between the resurrection of Jesus and Christian beliefs about life after death	Learning about religion: a, b, e, h Learning from religion: a, c, e Themes: e, f, h, i, Experiences and opportunities: p, q
What do Christians believe happens when someone dies?	To reflect on the story of the water bugs and dragonflies as an allegory that helps us to understand what Christians believe about life after death	Learning about religion: a, b, e, f Learning from religion: c Themes: a, h, i Experiences and opportunities: p, q
A place of rest	To know that a graveyard is a place where people are buried To understand that people find it comforting to visit a graveyard and remember those who have died	Learning about religion: b Learning from religion: a, Themes: k Experiences and opportunities: p
A graveyard with a difference	To understand that graveyards are not all alike around the world To consider that graves can tell us about the people who have died	Learning about religion: a, b, d, e Learning from religion: a, Themes: g, h, i, l Experiences and opportunities: p
Going to a Christian funeral	To know some of what happens at a Christian funeral To understand that this is a time of sadness and also of sharing good memories To understand that a hospice is a place that supports someone who is dying and their family	Learning about religion: a, b, e Learning from religion: a, c Themes: e, f, h, i Experiences and opportunities: p
Marking an end and celebrating a life	To understand that the state funeral of Queen Elizabeth, the Queen Mother, was both a public and a personal expression of sadness and pride	Learning about religion: a, d, e Learning from religion: a, b, Themes: g, h, i, l Experiences and opportunities: p, q
Helping us to remember	To reflect on the need to celebrate the lives of those who have died To appreciate that items that had significance to the person who has died help us to remember him/her	Learning about religion: b, e Learning from religion: a Themes: k Experiences and opportunities: p
Writing focus: My life journey	To reflect on and consider their own lives as a journey and their ability to shape the quality of the experience	Learning from religion: a, b, c, d, e Themes: h Experiences and opportunities: p

Glosssary

BUDDHISM

Buddha	*Awakened* or *Enlightened One*
Karma	*Action*. Intentional actions that affect a person's circumstances in this and future lives
Siddartha Gautama	The personal name of the Buddha

CHRISTIANITY

Alleluia/Hallelujah	A joyful expression used in Hebrew worship, meaning 'Praise the Lord'. Christian liturgies often use it, particularly at Easter. The 'Hallelujah Chorus' is the concluding piece of Part II of Handel's *Messiah*
Baptism	A rite of initiation involving immersion in, or sprinkling or pouring of, water
Baptistry/baptistery	(i) Building or pool used for baptism, particularly by immersion (ii) Part of a church where baptism takes place
Bishop	The most senior member of the clergy, in charge of a diocese
Confirmation	A Christian rite admitting a baptised person to full membership of a church
Dedication	A rite or ceremony of dedicating
Eucharist	*Thanksgiving*. A service celebrating the sacrificial death and resurrection of Jesus Christ, using elements of bread and wine. Sometimes called the Lord's Supper or Holy Communion
Font	Receptacle to hold water used in baptism
Godparent	A person who sponsors someone (the godchild) at baptism; supporter of the spiritual development of the godchild until old enough to take responsibility personally
Holy Communion	*see* Eucharist
Holy Spirit	The third person of the Holy Trinity. Active as divine presence and power in the world, and dwelling in believers to make them like Christ and empower them to do God's will
Immersion	Baptism performed by totally submerging a person in water
Mass	Term for the Eucharist, used by the Roman Catholic Church and others
Miracle	An event that appears inexplicable by the laws of nature and so is held to be supernatural in origin or an act of God
Priest	In many Christian churches, a member of the clergy ranking below a bishop but above a deacon and having authority to administer the sacraments
Rector	The priest of a parish in the Church of England – generally a term used in country areas
Resurrection	(i) The rising from the dead of Jesus Christ on the third day after the crucifixion (ii) The rising from the dead of believers at the Last Day
Vicar	The priest of a parish in the Church of England
Vow	A promise to perform a specified act or behave in a certain manner

HINDUISM

Atman	*Self*. Can refer to the body, mind or soul; it refers to the real self, the soul
Brahmin	The first of the four *varnas*, the principal social groupings from which priests are drawn
Ganesh	Hindu deity portrayed with an elephant's head - a sign of strength. The deity who removes obstacles
Ganges	Most famous of all sacred rivers of India
Hanuman	Monkey warrior who faithfully served Rama and Sita
Hindu	A follower of the Hindu faith
Krishna	An avatar of Vishnu. His teachings are found in the Bhagavad Gita
Mandir	Either a temple or a household shrine. Often called a Kovil in South India
Moksha	Ultimate liberation from the continuous cycle of birth and death
Ramayana/Ramayan	The Hindu epic that relates the story of Rama and Sita, composed thousands of years ago
Rama/Ram	The incarnation of God, and hero of the Ramayana. Ram is pronounced 'Rarm' to rhyme with 'arm', not 'Ram' to rhyme with 'tram'
Ravana/Ravan	Evil demon king who kidnapped Sita and bore her away to his kingdom in Lanka
Reincarnation	The belief that when someone dies, although the body decomposes, something is reborn in another body. It is the belief that someone has lived before and will live again in another body after death
Sita	Wife and consort of Rama
Varanasi	City on the river Ganges, sacred to Shiva. It is one of the holiest Hindu pilgrimage sites

ISLAM

Allah	The name for God in Arabic and used in preference to the English word 'God' by Muslims. This Arabic term is singular, has no plural, nor it is associated with masculine or feminine characteristics. Arab Christians also call God 'Allah'
Allah u Akbar	'Allah is most great.'
Islam	Peace attained through willing obedience to Allah's divine guidance
Muslim	One who claims to have accepted Islam by professing the Shahadah
Qur'an	That which is read or recited. The Divine Book revealed to the Prophet Muhammad (pbuh). Allah's final revelation to humankind

JUDAISM

Bar mitzvah	*Son of Commandment*. A boy's coming of age at 13 years old, usually marked by a synagogue ceremony and family celebration
Bat mitzvah	*Daughter of Commandment*. As above, but for girls from 12 years old. This may be marked differently between communities
Hebrew	Ancient Semitic language; language of the Hebrew Scriptures and used by Jews for prayer and study. Everyday language in Israel
Huppah/chuppah	Canopy used for a wedding ceremony, under which the bride and groom stand
Kippah	Small, round head-covering worn by Jewish men and boys
Mazel tov	Good luck
Rabbi	*My teacher*. An ordained Jewish teacher
Synagogue	A Jewish place of worship
Torah	The first five books of the Hebrew Bible: Genesis, Exodus, Leviticus, Numbers and Deuteronomy
Yad	Hand-held pointer used in reading the Sefer Torah

SIKHISM

Amrit	*Nectar*. Sanctified liquid made of sugar and water, used in initiation ceremonies
Baisakhi	(also spelt *Vaisakhi*) A major Sikh festival celebrating the formation of the Khalsa in 1699
Gurdwara	(also spelt *Gurudwara*) *The doorway to the Guru*. Sikh place of worship.
Granthi	Reader of the Guru Granth Sahib, who officiates at ceremonies
Guru	*Teacher*. In Sikhism, the title of Guru is reserved for the ten human Gurus and the Guru Granth Sahib
Guru Gobind Singh	(also called *Guru Govind Singh*). The Tenth Sikh Guru. It is important to note that the title 'Guru' must be used with all the Gurus' names
Guru Granth Sahib	Primal collection of Sikh scriptures
Kaccha/Kachera	Traditional underwear/shorts
Kangha	Comb worn in the hair
Kara	Steel band worn on the right wrist
Kaur	Princess. Name given to all Sikh females by Guru Gobind Singh
Kesh	Uncut hair
Khalsa	The community of the pure. The Sikh community
Khandra	Double-edged sword used in the initiation
Kirpan	A small sword – 'dagger' should be avoided
Panj Pyare	The Five Beloved Ones. Those first initiated into the Khalsa and their representatives today
Singh	*Lion*. Name adopted by Sikh males
The Five Ks	The five main symbols of Sikh commitment

Acknowledgements

All video material is sourced from the BBC, with the exception of *Baptism in a Baptist church* (courtesy of the Baptist Union of Great Britain) and *Marriage vows* (a home video).

All images not credited are from the BBC.

Every effort has been made to clear copyright within this resource. In instances where we may have failed to do so, we will be happy to rectify this at the first opportunity.

Page title	Description (photo/text/audio/artwork)	Source/acknowledgement
Growing old	Two elderly ladies	Martin Mayer/Alamy
	Man running the marathon	Dominic Burke/Alamy
	Two small boys	Photo Network/Alamy
	Three ladies at a tea dance	David Taylor/Alamy
	Group of surfers on the beach	Jim Wileman/Alamy
	Toddler in the garden	Angela Cannon
	Teenagers	Geoffrey Hammond/ iStockphoto
The start of life	Mother and baby	Marmion/iStockphoto
	Baby in cot	Gary Roebuck/Alamy
Writing focus: A big responsibility	Priest baptises a baby boy, with godparent	David Bratley/Alamy
Changes and new beginnings	School assembly	Ian Shaw/Alamy
	Mums picking up pupils from school	Bubbles Photolibrary/Alamy
	School rugby scrum	Janine Wiedel Photolibrary/Alamy
	School orchestra	Steve Skjold/Alamy
	School playground	Janine Wiedel Photolibrary/Alamy
	Secondary school pupils in uniform	Education Photos/Alamy
	Back of three pupils, Exeter	Kevin Clifford Photography/Alamy
	School athletics	Kim Karpeles/Alamy
A world of weddings	Wedding in Japan	Peter Horree/Alamy
	Wedding in Ethiopian Orthodox Tewahedo Church	Janine Wiedel Photolibrary/Alamy
	Wedding in Peru, Lake Titicaca	Images&Stories/ Alamy
	Wedding in the Fiji Islands	Hemis/Alamy
	Traditional Greek church wedding	terry harris just greece photolibrary/Alamy
	Hindu wedding, Sri Lanka	Peter Horree/Alamy
	Wedding in Bali	Peter Horree/Alamy
	Women dancing at a wedding celebration in Tanzania	blickwinkel/Alamy
The end of this life's journey	View over field towards Falstone village, Northumberland (winter)	Leslie Garland Picture Library/Alamy
	View over field towards Falstone village, Northumberland (spring)	Leslie Garland Picture Library/Alamy
	View over field towards Falstone village, Northumberland (summer)	Leslie Garland Picture Library/Alamy
	View over field towards Falstone village, Northumberland (autumn)	Leslie Garland Picture Library/Alamy
The story of Kisa and the mustard seeds	Buddha with candles	Brian Chase/ iStockphoto
	Buddha temple	Martyn Unsworth/iStockphoto
	Bronze Buddha's face	Thaddeus Robertson/iStockphoto
Writing focus: My life jouney	Winding road through Canola Fields	AVTG/iStockphoto